Original title:
Peachy Days Ahead

Copyright © 2025 Creative Arts Management OÜ
All rights reserved.

Author: Colin Harrington
ISBN HARDBACK: 978-1-80586-440-0
ISBN PAPERBACK: 978-1-80586-912-2

The Light Beyond the Gloom

When skies are gray and spirits droop,
A rubber chicken starts to loop.
The sun appears, just like a joke,
And laughter dances, on the stroke.

A squirrel in shades, with snacks galore,
Does cartwheels while I check the floor.
The world is bright, a silly show,
With giggles bursting, oh, what a glow!

Afternoon Dreams in Bloom

In afternoon's soft, quirky glow,
The flowers whisper, 'Come and go!'
A daisy dons a funny hat,
While bees buzz past, chasing a cat.

The sunbeams tickle every leaf,
While butterflies do pirouette for relief.
A picnic spreads with sandwiches wide,
But ants plan on a sneaky ride!

A Tidal Wave of Cheer

A wave of laughter crashes down,
With clowns and giggles all around.
Seagulls dance to a silly tune,
While fish wear hats, and bubbles swoon.

The ocean sparkles with delight,
As jellybeans take off in flight.
Corny jokes float on the tide,
In this merry ride, I abide.

Hues of Happiness

Colors splatter on the wall,
A canvas made for one and all.
A purple cat, a greenish dog,
They join the dance, a merry fog.

Rainbows giggle, sliding by,
While cotton candy fills the sky.
In this palette of pure fun,
Who knew that joy could weigh a ton?

Warmth of the Season's Embrace

Sunshine spills like jelly on toast,
Silly hats become the new host.
Ice cream cones dance in the breeze,
Joyful laughter floats with ease.

Picnics hide ants in a heap,
Squirrels clash while we all peep.
Seashells chat with waves so loud,
Clouds wear smiles, fluffy and proud.

Dreams in Vibrant Shades

Crayons color outside the lines,
Whimsical grapes trade their vines.
Skateboards whiz with a loud cheer,
Kites flirting high, no sign of fear.

Tiny bugs throw a dance party,
Waltzing around, never tardy.
Daisies wear sunglasses all day,
Tickling socks in a playful fray.

Soft Whispers of Summer

Butterflies giggle in the air,
Telling secrets, beyond compare.
Watermelons wearing sun hats,
Join in chorus with silly chats.

Swing sets creak, a joyful sound,
While sprinkle donuts spin around.
Giggling raindrops make a splash,
Summer's here; oh, what a bash!

Golden Hours Await

Sunset paints the sky so bold,
Tales of magic yet untold.
S'mores turn sticky, a friendly goo,
Frogs in chorus sing out "moo."

Breezy whispers tease your hair,
Wishing stars begin to dare.
With every laugh, the world is bright,
Golden moments, pure delight.

Embracing Tomorrow's Glow

Tomorrow's bright, let's wear a grin,
For silly dances, let the fun begin!
With mismatched socks and hats askew,
We'll strut a line or two, just me and you.

The future's ours, a wobbly ride,
Like crabs on roller skates, side by side.
We'll giggle loud and trip with flair,
In silly shades, we'll dodge the glare.

Sunlit Paths of Tomorrow

On sunlit streets, we'll ride a goat,
With clowns and tunes, let's keep afloat.
We'll limbo dance beneath the sun,
Chasing shadows, having fun.

A quirky hat for every sight,
We'll spot the moon in broad daylight.
With ice cream spills and joyful yells,
Our laughter rings like jingle bells.

Honeyed Hues of Dawn

As morning breaks, we'll wear pajamas,
And juggle fruit like mad iguanas.
With sticky hands and laughter loud,
We'll form a breakfast-loving crowd.

Toast will fly while eggs take flight,
In this tastiest morning fright.
We'll dance around with syrup grace,
And paint our faces, just in case!

Blossoms in the Breeze

The blossoms sway with laughter's tease,
As we embrace the playful breeze.
With flower crowns and silly songs,
We'll skip along where laughter throngs.

A bee will buzz, ask for a dance,
We'll spin and twirl, give it a chance.
With sprinkles on our heads, we'll play,
And make the most of this bright day.

Radiant Futures Unfold

The sun woke up with a silly grin,
It brushed its rays on everyone,
Chasing squirrels in a joyful dance,
While we giggled at their funny prance.

Butterflies wearing tiny hats,
Zooming by like fuzzy chats,
Each moment wrapped in cheerful cheer,
Time to shout, "Hooray!" and smear!

Joyful Kisses of Light

Spring is here with polka dots,
The flowers wear their happy spots,
A breeze that tickles, then makes me sneeze,
With laughter floating through the trees.

Clouds are marshmallows in the sky,
While giddy birds just flutter by,
They chirp a tune, a quirky beat,
As we dance around on clumsy feet.

A Tapestry of Blissful Moments

Ice cream cones melting in the sun,
Oh, the mess is half the fun!
With sprinkles flying here and there,
It's a confetti fight, we don't care!

Silly selfies with goofy grins,
Reflect what all this joy begins,
We toast to days of likes and laughs,
In the crazy photo drafts.

The Sweetness of Anticipation

Jellybeans rain from the clouds above,
Oh sweet time, how we love!
With gummy bears as our guides in town,
We bounce around like a silly clown.

Planning parties with pie in the sky,
Cupcakes, balloons, oh my!
Every giggle fuels the light,
We'll celebrate from morning to night.

Pastel Pathways

Walking on clouds of cotton candy,
Giggles and smiles, oh so dandy.
Silly hats and mismatched shoes,
Dancing with squirrels, spreading the news.

Jellybean rainbows fill the sky,
Chasing dreams that float on by.
A world of whimsy, full of cheer,
Silly faces drawing near.

Joyful Wanderings

Bouncing through fields of bubble gum,
Everyone laughing, oh what fun!
Chasing after a wobbly kite,
Twisting and twirling with delight.

Jumping in puddles of lemon zest,
A race with ducks, who's the best?
Hands full of cookies, hearts full of glee,
Life is a circus, come join me!

Sunbeam Serenade

Singing tunes with the dancing breeze,
Sunshine tickles through the trees.
Hopping along on banana peels,
Each step brings laughter and squeals.

A parade of frogs in silly hats,
Playing the conga with chubby cats.
Whistling tunes with a lollipop,
Not a care and we won't stop!

Colors of Tomorrow

Painting skies in polka dot hues,
Swirling ice cream in vibrant blues.
Fruit-flavored clouds raining sprinkles,
High-fiving neighbors, sharing winks and twinkles.

Pancakes flipping in the morning sun,
Ticklish toes—oh, what fun!
With laughter and joy, we'll never tire,
Let's light up the world with our wild desire!

Soft Suns and Soft Smiles

The sun peeks out, a cheeky grin,
Wiggling toes, letting fun begin.
Silly hats on our heads so bright,
Dance like nobody's watching, what a sight!

Giggling clouds float overhead,
Jumping puddles, splashing ahead.
We chase the shadows, they can't hide,
In this bliss, we take a ride!

Garden of Morning's Glory

Waking blooms in colors loud,
Nature's laughter, oh so proud.
Bees like comedians, buzzing near,
Flipping petals, spreading cheer!

Squirrels chatter in their play,
Plotting mischief for the day.
The sun bathes us in warmth so keen,
In the garden, joy is seen!

Days of Sweet Laughter

Ice cream drips on chins of glee,
Giggles echo, wild and free.
Bubblegum clouds float in the sky,
Tickling fancies as they pass by!

We hop on swings, reaching for dreams,
Swinging on laughter, bursting at the seams.
With friends beside, the world's a show,
Every moment, laughter's glow!

Harvest of Happy Moments

Running through fields, legs like springs,
Catching fireflies, how the heart sings!
Jars of giggles, stacked high with care,
Sprinkling sunshine everywhere!

When candy rains from cotton skies,
We lick our lips, with joyful sighs.
The harvest's ripe, let's celebrate,
With every chuckle, we create fate!

Sunlit Horizons

The sun is shining, what a sight,
My cat is prancing, quite a fright.
The squirrels dance upon the lawn,
While I just sit, and munch my brawn.

A lemonade stand with funky hats,
Selling drinks to chubby rats.
The world is bright, with laughter loud,
In my town, we're very proud.

Nectar Dreams

I dreamed of honey, sticky, sweet,
With dancing bees upon my feet.
A bear in shades, so suave and cool,
He taught me how to break the rules.

We flew on kites made out of bread,
And sailed on boats with fishes' heads.
The stars were laughing, what a joke,
While I just giggled, choked on smoke.

Beneath the Blossom Tree

Underneath that fragrant bough,
I spotted ants in tiny rows.
They marched around, like little troops,
While I just laughed at their goofs.

A dog named Rufus wore a tie,
He thought he could fly, oh my, oh my!
We held a party, snacks galore,
With doggy music, what a roar!

Radiant Tomorrow

Tomorrow's bright with gigs and fun,
There's a parade, it's just begun.
A clown named Chuck with wobbly shoes,
Will juggle pies and spread the blues.

The ice cream truck will blare its tune,
While kids all dance beneath the moon.
With sprinkles flying, giggles wide,
Life is golden, let's enjoy the ride.

Uplifted by the Wind

A feather in a breezy tune,
Soaring high, we'll leave by noon.
With kites that dance like silly ducks,
Chasing laughter, just our luck!

Socks on feet and slips on floors,
Ice cream spills and candy wars.
We'll find our joy in every gust,
Floating dreams, it's a must!

The Golden Voyage Awaits

Jump aboard a pirate ship,
With jellybeans and soda sips.
We'll sail through marshmallow skies,
Wearing cupcakes as our prize!

The treasure map, it leads us near,
To cotton candy, never fear!
With every wave and giggle loud,
Our silly crew, we are so proud!

Echoes of a Bright Tomorrow

In a world where laughter sings,
The sun wears shades, it's quite the thing!
Birds sing ballads of delight,
While we frolic into the night!

Upside-down and side by side,
We'll roll through life with goofy pride.
Bouncing on our pogo sticks,
Cracking jokes, and cheesy tricks!

Daydreams Beneath the Blush

Under skies of berry pink,
We'll sip on smoothies, have a wink.
Worms wear hats and dance in style,
It's all quite silly, let's stay awhile!

Riding bicycles with a horn,
Chasing rainbows since the morn.
With giggles loud and hearts so bright,
We'll make the world our own delight!

Sweet Serendipity

Life's a pie with a slice so sweet,
Oops! I tripped over my own two feet.
Falling into laughter, what a sight,
Bouncing back up, everything feels right.

Sunshine spills like juice on the floor,
While squirrels dance, knocking at my door.
With every hiccup, joy finds a way,
Who knew clumsiness was here to stay?

From Petals to Possibilities

Bumbling bees buzz with silly grace,
Chasing away clouds, just in case.
Flowers giggle in the gentle breeze,
Waving hello to the bumblebees.

My hat's so big it flies like a kite,
When the wind blows, what a funny sight!
Petals scatter, I'm covered in bloom,
Yet here I stand, embracing the gloom!

Canvas of Bright Beginnings

A paintbrush slips, splattering blue,
Turns out green was the goal, who knew?
Colors mingle with a cheerful splat,
As I grumble, "This doesn't look like that!"

Sticky fingers and a stained old tee,
Artistry is tricky, oh goodie me!
Each stroke a giggle, a joyful art,
Who knew silly blunders would warm my heart?

A Garden of Endless Possibilities

In a garden filled with wild ideas,
Rabbits wear bowties, defying fears.
Gnomes breakdance under the shining sun,
While plants whisper jokes, oh what fun!

Each weed I pulled led to laughter loud,
Unexpected blooms, I felt so proud.
With every twist and turn I take,
This garden thrives on each silly mistake!

Trails of Contented Wander

In fields where laughter runs so free,
We'll dance like squirrels, just you and me.
With candy skies and jellybean streams,
We'll frolic along, living our dreams.

And if a cloud shouts, 'Rain, oh dear!',
We'll spin our umbrellas, give a cheer.
For puddles are just nature's big pools,
Where every splash makes us feel like fools.

Unfolding Happiness

Balloons tied to a grinning cat,
Chasing its tail, oh what's up with that?
Each twist and turn brings giggles galore,
As ice cream drips down to the floor.

A pie in the face? Well, that's just grand!
It's all part of life's big splatty plan.
With whipped cream dreams and laughter's charms,
We'll gather the fun in happy arms.

Serenades of Sunny Surprises

A squirrel in shades, strumming his tune,
Under a bright, smiling orange moon.
He plays for the bees and the flowers dressed,
In polka dots, they jiggle, all impressed.

Lollipop clouds float by in array,
Dropping sprinkles on this sunny play.
With every buzz and every cheer,
We'll dance in circles, let go of fear.

Life's Sweet Symphony

A symphony of giggles fills the air,
As we ride on a swing, without a care.
With twirling hats and shoes that squeak,
Each moment we share turns rosy and chic.

The world is a stage, with slips and falls,
We juggle our joys, but not the balls.
In harmony with the hiccups and sighs,
We'll laugh till we pop like bright pie flies!

The Dawn of New Adventures

Awake, I rise with morning cheer,
The sun is bright, no hint of fear.
Socks mismatched, a silly sight,
I dance around, feeling just right.

Trips to the park with a picnic in tow,
I've packed a sandwich, but where did it go?
Found in my bag with a squished up snack,
It's a lunch that's sure to make me crack!

A squirrel stops by, he's eyeing my treat,
He looks so bold, I'm quick on my feet.
I toss him a grape, he gives me a wink,
Guess he agrees, it's fun to rethink!

Under the trees, the laughter does soar,
As friends join in, we giggle and roar.
Life's little quirks keep us all amused,
With silly antics, we'll never be bruised!

Vibrant Journeys

Rollerskating in my socks,
Chasing clouds that giggle and mock.
Sunshine wraps me in a bear hug,
As I dance with a plump little bug.

Lemonade rivers, oh what a glee,
Surprise water fights, come join me!
We'll toast to wild hats and silly shoes,
Life's a circus, let's share the news!

The ice cream truck sings a jolly tune,
I'm twirling like a bright balloon.
With sprinkles raining from the sky,
Who knew happiness could fly so high?

So grab your cap, and let's collide,
On this ride of laughter, side by side.
No maps are needed for this craze,
Just joyful hearts that want to play!

Bursting with Joy

Frothing bubbles in my mug,
Dancing like a wiggly bug.
Catch the cake, it's flying high,
Oh dear, why did I even try?

Confetti rain from above,
Shouting out my heartfelt love.
With jellybeans and gummy ducks,
Who needs plans? Just random luck!

Chasing shadows, what a race,
Silly hats upon my face.
With every slide, a howl of cheer,
It's a carnival, come near!

Flip-flops squeak across the ground,
Where mess and laughter can be found.
Let's paint the sky in vibrant tones,
Screaming our joy in silly groans!

Fields of Light

Giggling daisies wave hello,
Tickling toes as I skip below.
Butterflies with tiny crowns,
Are laughing while the sunshine frowns.

Bumbles buzzing through the air,
Chasing giggles everywhere.
Rolling down a grassy hill,
What a ride, what a thrill!

Kites that whirl in crazy loops,
Doodle games with rainbow groups.
Every second drips with cheer,
Let's wrap it all in a hug, my dear!

When clouds roll in, we won't mind,
Let's make funny faces, we're one of a kind.
In fields of light, we'll frolic bold,
With laughter as our treasure, pure gold!

Savoring the Sunshine

Sunglasses perched upon my nose,
Sipping sunshine, that's how it goes.
With marshmallow clouds for my chair,
I float along without a care.

Ticklish grass where wildflowers sway,
I'll wear a daisy in my hair today.
Jumping puddles with rubber boots,
Cracking up with shining toots!

A picnic feast with jelly toast,
Goofy dances, we'll raise a toast.
Eating ice cream like it's a race,
Who needs a sunny face?

So let's swing high and let's spin low,
Laughing until our cheeks glow.
In this warmth, we won't be shy,
Let's savor moments as they fly!

Glimmers of Hope on the Horizon

A squirrel in shades, he's quite the sight,
Juggling acorns in broad daylight.
He winks and struts without a care,
Life's a circus, how rare!

The birds sing out in feathered tune,
While frogs practice their ballet under the moon.
Each splash is a laugh, oh what a show,
Keep your eyes peeled, don't be slow!

Even the flowers don party hats,
Bouncing up high, and no time for spats.
They giggle as bees do the cha-cha dance,
Nature's so wild, it's quite the romance.

So grab your shades and join the fun,
In this quirky world, there's room for everyone.
With joy in our hearts and laughter so near,
The horizon sparkles, nothing to fear.

Nature's Palette of Delight

A garden sprawls with colors bright,
The daisies whisper, oh what a sight!
Ladybugs wear polka dots as they twirl,
In this wild, wacky, floral swirl.

The sunflowers giggle, they shout and sway,
As butterflies fling confetti their way.
The grass tickles toes, a soft, green rug,
Life's a big hug, another snug mug!

Clouds wear crowns, floating with glee,
As rainbows paint smiles for you and me.
The tree branches dance with a musical flair,
Every critter joins in, without a care.

So scatter your worries, let laughter ignite,
Embrace the chaos, what pure delight!
In nature's palette, every stroke sings,
Joy is the magic that each moment brings.

Dancing on Cloud Nine

Socks mismatched, I'm ready to groove,
In a world where shufflers lose their move.
With twirls and spins, I whip and whirl,
    Even the cat joins, a dizzy swirl.

The sun shines bright, a disco ball high,
    While daisies bow as I slide by.
The ants form lines, a conga parade,
Even the old dog gets in the charade!

Butterflies flutter with sparkling flair,
    As I attempt my best aerial stare.
Falling face first in a pile of leaves,
    Laughter erupts, oh how it weaves!

So throw off your shoes, come join the spree,
    Dance like a noodle, wild and free.
On clouds of bliss, let's frolic and play,
    In this merry moment, hip-hip-hooray!

Sun-Kissed Horizons

With a hat too big, a smile so wide,
I strut down the street with no need to hide.
The sun is my companion, makes shadows dance,
As I prance around, lost in a trance.

Balloons float high in the bright blue sky,
A flock of dreams, oh me, oh my!
The ice cream melts, but there's laughter galore,
As sprinkles explode—who could want more?

Kites swoop low, then soar to the peak,
The wind's a good friend, never bleak.
Children giggle, as dogs bark with cheer,
In this sunny patch, all worries disappear.

With every ray, the world seems to beam,
In these golden hours, life feels like a dream.
So let's toast to the joy that never fades,
On sun-kissed horizons, let's dance in parades!

Garden of Whimsy

In the garden where oddities bloom,
Gnomes play chess while flowers make room.
Bees wear hats, quite fancy and bright,
Chasing the sun in whimsical flight.

Daisies gossip with the sneaky breeze,
While laughing tomatoes drop down with ease.
A squirrel serenades with a funky tune,
Under the glow of a giggling moon.

Breezy Bliss

On a swing made of old yogurt lids,
Cats spin donuts while dancing skids.
Clouds drape like cotton candy puffs,
As wind tickles toes and leaves in cuffs.

A yellow chick wears shades of bright blue,
Grinning as if it's got jokes for you.
Lemonade rivers flow with a splash,
While marigold fish do a splashes dash.

Silhouettes of Joy

Jester shadows play tag in the dusk,
Tickling the stars with laughter and musk.
Balloons pull the moon into a sweet race,
While fireflies join in, lighting the space.

The trees have tales that make locals chuckle,
Whispering secrets in soft, leafy huddles.
Merry-go-rounds spin on the tips of trees,
Giggles turn into gold, if you please.

Tender Hues of Harmony

A wild dance where colors collide,
Purple hippos play peek-a-boo with pride.
Sunshine tickles a shy dandelion,
While cumulus clouds become a lion.

Bananas in hats host a fruity parade,
As maraschino cherries are happily made.
Each splash of paint bursts with a cheer,
In this happy world, joy is the premier.

Dawn of a Loving Radiance

The sun peeks out with a wink,
Coffee brews, eyes start to blink.
Socks mismatched, a grand fashion show,
Laughing at chaos, letting it flow.

Birds chirp tunes that sound quite silly,
Sipping juice, feeling so frilly.
Toast does a dance, it's ready to eat,
Morning's a party, can't be beat!

Rain clouds might try to crash this spree,
But umbrellas are hats, wait and see!
Splish-splash walks turn giggles to glee,
In this playful breeze, we're all free!

With ice cream dreams and sprinkles galore,
Happiness knocks on every door.
Life's a jester in colorful play,
Come join the fun, let's laugh away!

A Daydreamer's Delight

Floating on clouds of whipped-up cream,
Chasing after a sugary dream.
Pineapple pizza? What a bizarre thrill!
Dancing with lollipops, such a sweet skill.

The cat wears shades, sleeping with flair,
While I juggle lemons without a care.
What's on the agenda? Just silliness,
Sweaters with shorts, make a fashion mess!

Time is an octopus, waving its arms,
Tickling our toes with its funny charms.
Wherever we go, we'll walk the fine line,
Between dreams and giggles, oh how we shine!

A parade of socks dances down the street,
Scents of mischief and candy we greet.
So grab your laughter, it's time to ignite,
In this day of whims, we'll hold on tight!

Aromas of Serene Mornings

Whiskers twitch as breakfast does sizzle,
Coffee's brisk, but the toast has a drizzle.
Cereal dives into milk with cheer,
Mornings are messy, but so very dear.

Sunshine spills like syrup on pancakes,
Jam on the floor, but who really wakes?
In this cozy chaos, smiles come alive,
Finding the joy, and here we thrive!

A yoga mat? It's a wrestling ring,
As cats act like they're the ultimate king.
Downward dog? More like downward flop,
In our happy home, we never stop!

Laughter's the tune that fills every room,
With silly hats, we banish the gloom.
Set the table with giggles today,
In aromas of joy, we'll find our way!

Picturesque Pathways Ahead

Stepping outside in a bouncy gait,
The sidewalk sways, a dance we create.
Butterflies giggle, colors awake,
The world is art, make no mistake!

With lemonade stands and feathery hats,
Chasing the clouds that turn into cats.
Picnic plans with mustard and bread,
Who knew a sandwich could spin in my head?

Stumbling upon a magical street,
Where caramel rivers flow to our feet.
Skipping the stones that sing us a song,
Creating a melody where we belong.

The bike wheels whirl, we're off on a quest,
In whimsical lands where laughter's the best.
So grab your dreams, let's play pretend,
On this picture-perfect joy that won't end!

Winds of Change and Cheer

The breeze is giggling, oh so light,
It tickles the trees, a joyful sight.
Socks are mismatched, and shoes are bright,
We dance like daisies in pure delight.

Clouds wear smiles, not a care to fret,
Sunshine's a prankster, don't you forget.
Laughter is tangled, like spaghetti wet,
In this joyful whirlwind, we won't regret.

Glowing Vistas

Daffodils blush in the morning sun,
They wiggle with joy, oh what fun!
Bumblebees buzzing, a honking run,
A garden of laughter has just begun.

Rainbows are sliding, just like a game,
With colors that dance, and never the same.
We paint our troubles with glimmers of fame,
Each day a canvas, no two are the same.

Chasing the Last Golden Rays

The sun is winking, nearing its rest,
Chasing shadows, we feel so blessed.
Flip-flops squeaking, a funny quest,
Catching the light, we're truly obsessed.

Ice cream drips down our eager hands,
We race with giggles, across the sands.
Seagulls are laughing, making their plans,
In sunset's glow, we're the happiest bands.

Life's Orchard of Delight

Fruit flies are dancing, what a grand show,
Each apple's a giggle, each pear a glow.
Silly squirrels plotting, with seeds in tow,
In this orchard of laughter, let your heart grow.

Breezes bring whispers from branches so high,
Each bloom is a chuckle, a pink-scented sigh.
With every ripe joke, we reach for the sky,
In fields full of giggles, we'll never be shy.

Vibrant Echoes of Bliss

The sun's a giant lemon slice,
Bouncing on our heads, oh nice!
Ice cream drips, a sticky race,
We laugh and giggle, what a place!

The birds all chirp in silly tones,
Dancing with their feathered bones.
Squirrels wear tiny party hats,
And join the fun with acrobat chats.

Clouds are candy—fluffy, sweet,
We chase them down, they can't be beat.
Jumping puddles in our shoes,
Get ready, world, for our big news!

With every laugh, the skies expand,
We spread our joy across the land.
These moments bright, like quirky art,
In vibrant echoes, we take part.

Threads of Contentment

Waking up with socks that clash,
I tumble out and make a splash.
The toast is burnt, the coffee's strong,
But oh, who says that's all wrong?

Cat steals my chair, what a charade,
I bribe him with a piece of jade.
Outside, the world is clad in cheer,
Join the parade, bring on the beer!

Dancing with my lunchbox friend,
We twist and twirl, who needs to mend?
With every bite, laughter begins,
In these threads, let the fun spin!

Socks unmatched, hair a wild nest,
In this chaos, we are blessed.
Content, we wander, smiles on our face,
In the weirdness, we find our place.

Breezy Adventures Await

The kite is stuck upon a tree,
My neighbor yells, 'That's not for me!'
Chasing dreams on a skateboard,
We bump and crash, our spirits soared!

Mismatched shoes on this fine day,
We skip like frogs in a ballet.
The wind whispers secrets in my ear,
A treasure map is drawing near!

Hot dogs flying in the sun,
Laughing at our lunchtime fun.
With every step, another plot,
On adventures that can't be bought.

Chasing stars with a paper plane,
Through laughter's door, we break the chain.
With breezy bursts of joy, we play,
Together, we seize the day!

Effervescent Days Ahead

Bubbles bounce in fizzy cheer,
We pop and laugh, that's how we steer.
Sprinkler fights in the summer rain,
Oh, what fun is there to gain!

Chasing friends on sticky grass,
Silly races; who'll be last?
We trip and roll, like clowns on stage,
Creating giggles, page by page.

Riding bikes with wobbly grace,
Bikes to nowhere, it's our space.
In a sea of ice-cream dreams,
Life is better than it seems!

Oh, effervescence fills our hearts,
As sunshine dances, joy imparts.
With laughter as our loyal thread,
We toast to all that lies ahead!

The Fruitful Path Awaits

In a garden of giggles, we explore,
Chasing butterflies that dance and soar.
With every step, a joke we find,
Tickles and chuckles, we're intertwined.

Beneath the trees, we spot a snail,
He wears a hat, oh what a tale!
A fruity feast, we've got our plan,
For every laugh, we'll need a fan.

A runaway peach rolls down the lane,
With a voice like thunder, it starts to complain.
"Why do they giggle? I'm just a fruit!"
We howl with laughter, this prank's a hoot.

So hand in hand, with humor in bloom,
We'll skip through fields, dispelling gloom.
On this fruitful path, let's laugh and play,
Tomorrow's smiles start right today!

Golden Hour Gleam

When the sun sets low and the world turns light,
We gather for laughs, what a silly sight!
With glasses of juice and cookies galore,
In this goofy twilight, who could ask for more?

A squirrel does a dance on a bright yellow ball,
We cheer him on, he's having a ball!
In the glow of the sunset, we sing a tune,
While crickets play drums, and daisies swoon.

Our shadows stretch wide, like our hopes and dreams,
We tumble and giggle as sunlight beams.
A picnic of delight, with marshmallows bold,
We toast to the stories that never get old.

As the golden hour wraps us in cheer,
We'll laugh 'til we cry, forgetting our fear.
With each silly stunt and cheesy joke,
We find brighter days wrapped in laughter's cloak.

Laughter in the Breeze

Amidst the tall trees, the wind whispers sweet,
It carries our laughter, a rhythmic beat.
With kites in the air, we dance in the sun,
Each moment a treasure, each giggle a pun.

A puppy races past, with a hat on his head,
We burst into fits, unable to tread.
His goofy antics have won our hearts,
In the laughter-filled air, no one departs.

Oh, who knew the grass was so soft for a fall?
We tumble and roll, our joy's a free-for-all.
With bubbles that float high, we chase them with glee,
A breeze full of fun, just you and me.

As day turns to dusk, we gather our cheer,
In the laughter of breezes, we have nothing to fear.
Let's bottle these giggles, let's share the delight,
For humor and friendship make everything bright!

Blooming Possibilities

In a world of bloom, where laughter's the key,
We wander the paths, just you and me.
With flowers that giggle and bees that smile,
We'll chase our dreams, if just for a while.

A daisy winks, a rose tells a joke,
The sun spills its gold, as if it's bespoke.
With every new petal, a story unfolds,
In this garden of laughter, our joy is bold.

We play hopscotch on clouds overhead,
And bounce on the laughter that fills us instead.
A butterfly giggles, "Don't take life too serious!"
We twirl and we leap, it can't get delirious.

So here's to the blooms and the fun in the air,
With friends by our side, we've nothing to spare.
Each moment's a blossom that bursts with delight,
In this garden of giggles, we'll dance through the night!

Inspiring Ripples of Radiance

A squirrel in a bowtie, what a sight,
He dances like it's Saturday night.
With acorns and dreams, he spins around,
Making the forest feel magic-bound.

The sun in the sky winks with a grin,
While birds in bands start to sing in.
A raccoon with shades, oh what a champ,
He's hosting a party by the lamp!

Breezes swirl laughter, tickling the trees,
As frogs wear crowns, hopping with ease.
Each ripple of joy sends giggles and glee,
Nature's own circus, wild and free.

In the pond, the frogs dive with flair,
Cannonballs splash! Water everywhere.
The world spins and twirls in sweet delight,
A carnival of colors, oh what a sight!

Fields of Color and Light

In fields where the daisies have a chat,
A potato dressed up like a fur-hatted brat.
Butterflies flutter in tulle and lace,
Joining the dance, oh what a grace!

Sunflowers gossip in towering ranks,
While rabbits in shades paint their pranks.
With giggles that echo across the blue sky,
Even the clouds burst out laughing, oh my!

Pink pigs strut along on a parade,
With fabulous hats that never will fade.
Piglets tumble, roll in a jig,
Creating a scene so wonderfully big!

The laughter bounces from tree to tree,
As ducks play poker with chips made of pea.
In this colorful realm of pure delight,
Every moment shines with laughter so bright!

A Journey Wrapped in Warmth

A bear in a sweater takes the lead,
With honey on toast, oh what a feed.
They wander through forests, laughing together,
Under quilted skies, all light as a feather.

A turtle with style, a snail on skates,
In this whimsical world, everyone waits.
For tea with the fox, served in a cup,
Filled with dreams, and sweet laughter on tap!

They wander through valleys, all smiles and cheer,
Bananas wear hats, how funny, oh dear!
Each step is a giggle, each glance a delight,
In this curious dance, everything feels right.

Stars join the party, winking with flair,
While constellations tickle, floating in air.
They whisper of journeys wrapped in their glow,
Where warmth and joy continually flow!

Sunkissed Whispers of Joy

An octopus flirts, wearing polka dots,
With sunglasses perched while brewing hot pots.
In the sunlit waves, he does a twirl,
As fishes around him giggle and swirl.

A clam plays the violin under the sun,
His friends all applaud, what a magical fun!
The seaweed dances, sways side to side,
While bubbles of laughter glisten with pride.

Seagulls in fashion, sporting bow ties,
Swoop down to share some pie from the skies.
With pastry and cream, they toast with delight,
In this whimsical world, where all's sunny bright.

The tide rolls in, brings whispers, oh dear,
Smiling sea creatures, all gathered near.
Every wave drops a chuckle so clear,
In the sea of joy, nothing to fear!

The Cheer of Gentle Breezes

A breeze tickles our noses, oh what a tease,
It sways the trees with such playful ease.
The sun winks down with a golden glare,
And squirrels dance like they haven't a care.

Ice cream drips on a giggling chin,
We chase our shadows, let the fun begin!
Butterflies flutter, making us grin,
As laughter echoes, it's a joyful din.

The laughter flows like a bubbling brook,
While we tell tales from an old storybook.
With each silly joke, our sides start to ache,
These gentle breezes make our hearts quake.

So here's to the moments we seize in delight,
Where clouds seem to giggle and everything's bright.
In this carefree world, each laugh is a prize,
We're sunshine collectors, much to our surprise.

A Symphony of Blooming Joy

Flowers gossip in colors so bright,
They sway and they shimmy, a fanciful sight.
Each bloom sings a note, a sweet melody,
Creating a symphony, wild and free.

The bees are the dancers, swirling around,
In this garden of laughter, where joy can be found.
Petals wink at the clouds in the sky,
While the sun leans in, with a chuckle nearby.

With each prank of nature, we giggle and cheer,
As squirrels enact their acrobatic sphere.
Joy spills like lemonade on a hot summer's day,
Our hearts play the tunes, come what may!

So let's reach for the blossoms, let silly bloom,
With every petal, we banish the gloom.
A quirky garden where laughter won't end,
In this symphony of joy, we all can ascend.

Laughter in the Air

The air is filled with a sweet, silly sound,
As giggles and snickers twirl around.
The sun's bright grin complements the fun,
We race our shadows, daring the sun.

A flock of ducks in their waddly parade,
Quacking their jokes in a comical charade.
As the sky turns to canvas and splashes of blue,
Every moment here feels fresh and new.

Kites dance high in the whimsical breeze,
With faces aglow, we do what we please.
Chasing our laughter, our worries all fade,
In this carnival air, happiness is made.

So take a deep breath and join in the fun,
There's laughter awaiting under this sun.
With silly shenanigans filling our days,
We'll add joy in bundles, in whimsical ways.

Embracing Tomorrow's Glow

With a wink to the future, the sun starts to rise,
Kittens play tag as they pounce and they rise.
Balloons float gently, a colorful sight,
They giggle and bounce in the warm morning light.

Our dreams are like bubbles, so ready to soar,
Each wish is a spark, lighting up evermore.
With laughter like confetti, we'll dance in a row,
Embracing each moment, embracing the glow.

Jokes shared on the breeze are the best kind of treat,
As we trip on our shoelaces, we smile on our feet.
The future is bright, like a freshly made pie,
We'll savor the flavors, as time passes by.

So let joy be your compass, your heart be your map,
In this funny adventure, we'll never feel trapped.
With each giggle and guffaw, we'll hold on tight,
Embracing tomorrow, all shimmering and bright.

Sweet Embrace of Dawn

The sun peeks through with a cheeky grin,
Birds start chirping, let the fun begin!
Coffee spills, oh what a sight,
Morning dances, everything feels right.

Socks mismatched, a glorious mess,
Chasing the cat, oh what a stress!
Pancakes flip, syrup goes splat,
Laughter erupts, where's the dog at?

Jammies still on, we're all a sight,
Breakfast is chaos, what a delight!
Eggs on the ceiling, toast on the floor,
Who knew mornings could be such a chore?

But smiles abound, as we share the feast,
Together we rise, no worry, no least.
Sweet embrace of dawn, we're here to play,
It's another fine, goofy day!

Cotton Candy Skies

Above us puffs of pink and blue,
Clouds look like candy, it's all askew!
With lollipops swinging from tree to tree,
Who knew the sky could be so silly?

The sun's a giant gumdrop, shining bright,
While rainbows wiggle, what a funny sight!
Bubbles float by with a squeaky sound,
Tickling noses, joy unbound.

Kites caught in giggles, they dance and dive,
Chasing the breeze, like bees in a hive.
Swirling armfuls of laughter and cheer,
Cotton candy skies, we've nothing to fear!

So let's wear our hats, mismatched and wild,
Jump on the clouds, oh, let's be a child!
With laughter as loud as the chirping cheer,
Cotton candy skies bring us near!

Whispers of Summer's Kiss

Summer's here with a wink and a nudge,
Giggling flowers, they won't budge!
Watermelon slices, juicy and sweet,
Dance on the porch with flip-flops on feet.

Ice cream drips down my chin like a dream,
Sticky fingers, oh how we scream!
The sun plays peek-a-boo, all day long,
With lemonade sips, we can't go wrong.

Fireflies flash like tiny stars,
Chasing our laughter beneath the bars.
The moon wearing sunglasses, feeling so fine,
Whispers of summer, all yours and mine!

With laid-back breezes and hammock sways,
Every moment sparkles, in funny ways.
Life's one big joke, let's join the bliss,
In this summer's dance, with a touch of a kiss!

Juicy Promises

In the orchard, where laughter grows,
Fruits are hanging, in row after rows.
Bouncing with glee, we gather and munch,
Tasting the sweetness in every crunch.

Grapes getting giggly, what a delight,
With squirrels in coats, oh what a sight!
Cherries blushing, like kids on a swing,
Under this tree, oh what joy they bring!

Lemons laughing, so zesty and bright,
Juicy promises in every bite.
With juice running down, oh what a mess,
But happiness grows, I must confess!

So let's chase the flavors that dance in the air,
With fruits and giggles, nothing can compare.
Together we'll feast, with no care in sight,
Juicy promises, our hearts feeling light!

Warmth of a Sunbeam

A sunbeam tickles my nose,
It dances like a jolly prose.
With flipping pancakes, I glide,
And syrup spills like a joyride.

The birds are laughing in the trees,
Telling jokes carried by the breeze.
I chase my hat as it takes flight,
In this silly morning light.

Splashing puddles on my way,
Ring-a-ding, it's a playful day!
With laughter bubbling all around,
I hop and skip on joyful ground.

The cat joins in with a springy leap,
Chasing shadows while we peep.
In the warmth of this golden reign,
We'll celebrate, let the fun remain!

Sunkissed Adventures

With sunscreen slathered on my cheeks,
I'm ready for the sunny peaks.
Flip-flops clapping on the sand,
Every grain is a treasure planned.

Waves are laughing, splashing me,
I dive like a fish, oh so free!
Seagulls squawk with sassy flair,
I'll steal their chips, but they don't care.

A sandcastle rises, tall and proud,
As tourists stop and gather a crowd.
"Look at my kingdom!" I boast with glee,
As a rogue wave claims it, just wait and see!

Ice cream cones melt in the sun,
Sticky fingers add to the fun.
As evening falls, we toast the sky,
In this comedy where laughter can't die!

Orchard of Hope

In an orchard where the fruit does sway,
The squirrels plot their squirrelly play.
With baskets hung around my waist,
I'll race to gather all in haste.

Apples wobble on the trees,
Echoing laughter on a breeze.
Each one I pick is a fruity dance,
In this playful, harvest romance.

Bees buzz in their fuzzy suits,
Trying to steal my juicy fruits.
I wave them off, with a cheeky grin,
"Not today, my buzzed-out kin!"

With a pie on the table, warm and grand,
Each slice serves joy, hand in hand.
Family gathers with smiles so wide,
In this orchard, where fun can't hide!

Cerulean Bliss

Under the sky, so blue and bright,
I paint my dreams with sheer delight.
Clouds like marshmallows drift on by,
While I chase butterflies in the sky.

A kite flies high, dancing with glee,
It spirals down to visit me.
With giggles shared and jokes exchanged,
In this moment, nothing feels estranged.

Picnic blankets sprawled with care,
Sandwiches made with love to spare.
Ants march in a hilarious line,
Stealing snacks, thinking they're fine!

As the sun kisses the day goodnight,
Fireflies glow, a magical sight.
We laugh and play until we're sore,
In cerulean joy, we want more!

The Promise of Lush Horizons

With socks that clash and mismatched shoes,
I waltz through life, avoid the blues.
A squirrel stole my sandwich, quite the heist,
Yet laughter bubbles, oh what a feast!

The sun's my buddy, it shines so bright,
While I trip on grass, oh what a sight!
My coffee spills, a painting gone wrong,
But the tune of cheer is my favorite song.

Dancing with shadows, I spin and twirl,
What do you mean I can't be a girl?
A llama pops past, in shades of pink,
Life's silly moments, they make me think.

In this wild garden where creatures play,
I skip through puddles that shine like clay.
With each wacky step, I'm glad to roam,
These jolly mishaps feel just like home.

Sunbeams and Dreams

A sunbeam tickles my sleepy nose,
While I nibble breakfast, missed toast and froze.
Bananas in pajamas, a sight so rare,
I laugh at my dance, a wobbly flare.

Coffee's a friend, with sprinkles of fun,
But spill it on shoes, I'm now on the run!
Chasing my hat in a whirlwind spin,
This goofy adventure, I just can't win.

My cat walks by, as cool as a breeze,
With a flick of the tail, it knows how to tease.
A squirrel contests; who's ruler today?
The shenanigans shine, they're here to stay.

With colorful socks and mismatched flair,
I embrace the chaos, my wacky affair.
Sunshine and giggles, they light up my way,
These silly moments, they make me sway.

Bright Letters from Tomorrow

A letter arrived from tomorrow, I see,
It's written in pasta, how could that be?
It twirls and it twists, then dances about,
Yelling, 'Start laughing! No time for doubt!'

Flip-flops and wildflowers, such a mix,
Bringing my joy, like kaleidoscope tricks.
What's this? A goat in a tutu prances?
Na-na-na-na, my heart just dances!

Rain fell in colors, polka dot streams,
While ice cream sandwiches floated like dreams.
I raced with a penguin, all dressed in blue,
With silly confetti, oh what a view!

Stumbling on clouds, as grandkids would say,
Let laughter spill out, come what may.
Tomorrow's bright letters, in shades of delight,
Fill my world with joy, it feels just right.

Mosaic of Heartfelt Moments

In a world where bananas converse with the sun,
I munch on giggles, oh what a fun!
A snail in a bowtie, he dances with flair,
Spreading good vibes in the warm summer air.

Bubblegum clouds float high in the sky,
While birds wear sunglasses and swoop on by.
Tripping on laughter, I tumble and spin,
A goofy embrace, let the magic begin.

Pancakes stacked high on a table of dreams,
They giggle and wiggle, or so it seems.
With syrupy smiles and joy in the air,
This moment mosaic, a colorful flair.

Chasing my shadow around the green park,
With friends who are squirrels who each leave a mark.
Laughter's the glue that binds us so tight,
In these heartfelt moments, all feels so right.

www.ingramcontent.com/pod-product-compliance
Lightning Source LLC
Chambersburg PA
CBHW062109280426
43661CB00086B/400